DONNA LEON

The Iconic Biography of the Pen Queen of Venice

By

ICONIC PRESS

CONTENTS

INTRODUCTION

Donna Leon is prominent and highly regarded throughout the world for her fascinating crime novels featuring Commissario Guido Brunetti and set in the beautiful city of Venice amongst other writings. While Donna Leon's works have received international acclaim, she personally maintains a modest level of public visibility. As a result, not much is known about her and her life and effects have not been extensively explored. However, to that end, this book is created to give an overview of Donna Leon's past, work, personal life, interests, activism, and much more; as well as to throw light on the aspects that have contributed to her success in the literary world.

Donna Leon is known for her rigorous attention to detail, especially when describing the social, cultural, and political aspects of Venice in her mystery thrillers. She skillfully incorporates these components into engrossing tales that examine both the intricacy of Italian society and the criminal investigations carried out by Commissario Brunetti. Themes like corruption, the environment, and the futility of justice are all explored in depth in Donna Leon's books.

Although Donna Leon's works have received high appreciation, she is also known for her activism on behalf of several social and political causes. She is a fierce supporter of ecological preservation and has made a point of highlighting the value of conserving Venice's distinctive cultural history. Her commitment to these causes and her strong convictions give her craft an additional depth.

It is impossible to overestimate Donna Leon's contributions to the field of crime fiction and her influence as a writer, despite the fact that her private life is still mostly kept private. Millions of people around the world have read her books in many different languages, and a popular German television series was made from one of them. Her creative accomplishments have cemented her place among today's most cherished and recognized crime writers.

Donna Leon is renowned for both crime fiction and nonfiction books. Her writings are distinguished by their accurate portrayals of Venice and Italian society as well as by her ability to deftly incorporate the locations into her captivating plotlines. She made a huge addition to the field of crime fiction, and fans all around the world like her writing. She has influenced the entire world through her writings.

This is homage to a fiction author whose works continue to enthrall, inspire, and challenge readers all across the world. Discover the insights, motivations, and legendary intellect of one of our time's most renowned authors as you follow along on this engrossing voyage.

CHAPTER 1

BACKGROUND AND FORMATIVE YEARS

EARLY LIFE

Donna Leon, the acclaimed crime fiction author known for her Commissario Guido Brunetti series set in Venice, has led a fascinating life that has undoubtedly influenced her work. She was born on September 29, 1942, in Montclair, New Jersey, USA. She is the eldest daughter of two teachers and originally studied English Literature at the University of Florida and later went on to complete a doctorate in Renaissance Literature at the University of Maryland.

Her father, a Romance language teacher, was the one who introduced her to European literature and culture at a young age. This early exposure to the arts, as well as her father's influence, nourished her enthusiasm for books, laying the groundwork for her future writing endeavors.

Leon moved to Europe after graduating from the University of Maryland in the late 1960s. She first resided in Perugia, Italy, where she pursued her education and immersed herself in Italian culture. As she travelled over the country, she developed a great appreciation for its rich history, beautiful scenery, and distinct way of life. These events sparked her interest in Italy and inspired the picturesque backdrops of her crime books.

Leon relocated to Italy in the 1980s to work as an English Literature teacher for the University of Maryland's Overseas Division, where she taught American military men stationed there.

After leaving the institution, she worked as a lecturer at a local institution in Vicenza for several years.

Leon was eventually pulled to Venice, a city that would have an indelible impact on both her personal and professional life. Venice, with its labyrinthine canals, ageless beauty, and complicated social dynamics, served as the backdrop for her critically acclaimed series starring Commissario Guido Brunetti. Leon's stories incorporate the city's distinct appeal, as well as its history, cultural legacy, and modern challenges.

Prior to her career as a writer, Donna Leon held a variety of jobs and embarked on diverse interests. She was a tour guide in Rome and a teacher of English in Switzerland, Iran, China, and Saudi Arabia. These experiences gave her the opportunity to immerse herself in diverse cultures, obtain a better grasp of human dynamics, and sharpen her observational skills, all of which would later prove essential in building her complex characters and convoluted plotlines.

EDUCATION

Donna Leon's scholastic background has had a significant impact on her intellectual activities as well as the literary depth of her mystery books. While details about her education are few, it is apparent that her academic ambitions and intellectual curiosity have played a significant role in her development as an author. In this response, we will consider how Donna Leon's work and literary achievements were inspired by her education.

Donna Leon went to the University of Maryland after completing her primary and secondary education. Her exact topic of study at university is unknown, but her intellectual foundation provided her with critical thinking abilities and a well-rounded perspective.

Leon's love of literature and culture shines through in her novels, which represent her extensive knowledge of European literature and ancient classics, as well as her affinity for art forms like as opera. Her education most certainly contributed to her exposure to a wide range of literary works, which in turn influenced her approach to storytelling and characterization.

Furthermore, Leon's travels overseas and teaching experiences in numerous nations exposed her to a variety of cultures, languages, and social dynamics. These contacts with many societies improved her understanding of human behavior and equipped her with a multicultural perspective, which she expertly blends into her mystery novels.

While the specifics of Donna Leon's academic education are not widely known, her self-proclaimed love of reading and lifelong pursuit of knowledge have propelled her writing and intellectual endeavors. She has polished her talent as a crime fiction author by voracious reading and broad intellectual interest, producing sophisticated plots and multi-dimensional characters that mirror her intellectual depth.

Leon's formal and self-directed education has clearly nourished her creative imagination and equipped her with a solid basis for storytelling. Her complex portrayal of both the fanciful and true features of Venetian life demonstrates her ability to draw from a diverse range of cultural influences, literary traditions, and sociological observations.

Donna Leon's intellectual curiosity, absorption in European literature and culture, and teaching experiences have all played important roles in molding her as an author. Her commitment to lifelong learning, self-directed research, and the cultivation of

7

varied perspectives has enriched her mystery novels, allowing them to resonate with readers due to their depth, authenticity, and intellectual complexity. Leon shows how education, whether formal institutions or a lifetime pursuit of information, can help a writer's craft and the creation of captivating literary works.

CAREER BEGINNINGS

Donna Leon's writing career began with the publication of her debut novel, "Death at La Fenice," in 1992. This seminal novel established her as a leading voice in contemporary crime fiction. In my response, I'll go into great detail about Donna Leon's early years, the birth of her Commissario Guido Brunetti series, and the subsequent popularity.

Donna Leon worked as a scholar, a teacher, and an administrator before beginning her literary career. She rose up the ranks to become a literature professor at an American university. Leon cultivated her love of reading and gained a profound passion for storytelling and narrative craft while teaching in the United States.

Leon then relocated to Europe in the late 1960s, originally settling in Perugia, Italy. Her tour of the country, particularly her fascination with the city of Venice, served as the impetus for her switch from academia to writing and storytelling. The enchantment of Venice's canals, history, and cultural diversity, mixed with Leon's personal experiences and views, inspired her to start on a literary career centered on the city.

It was in Venice that Leon's path crossed with the birth of her iconic character, Commissario Guido Brunetti. Leon wrote a series of crime novels starring Brunetti as the protagonist, inspired by her passion for the city and her desire to investigate its geopolitical and cultural dynamics. The first novel in the series, "Death at La

8

Fenice," introduced readers to Brunetti's thorough and sympathetic approach to solving crimes in the unique environment of Venice.

The novel was an immediate success, attracting the attention of both readers and critics. It received great acclaim for its atmospheric representation of Venice, exquisite attention to detail, intriguing characters, and investigation of modern Italian social issues. The popularity of "Death at La Fenice" allowed Leon to build a dedicated readership eager to follow Brunetti's investigations against the backdrop of Venice's labyrinthine alleys and canals.

Following the success of the first novel, Donna Leon continued to write and publish further Brunetti novels, each adding to the series' depth and complexity. Her later books, such as "Death in Strange Country," "Acqua Alta," and "Fatal Remedies," cemented her position as a master of crime fiction. Leon displayed her ability to tackle both thought-provoking social topics and sophisticated, intriguing narratives, all while retaining a tight hold on Venice's distinct ambiance.

Donna Leon's career has been defined by a continuous output of Commissario Brunetti novels, expanding reputation, and worldwide success since its inception. Her books have been translated into other languages and have sold millions of copies worldwide. Her work has also been converted into a German television series, expanding her worldwide influence even further.

Donna Leon's career began when she moved from academics to the field of crime fiction writing, centered on the enthralling city of Venice. Her debut novel, "Death at La Fenice," was a runaway hit, paving the way for her enduring series starring Commissario Guido Brunetti. Leon's ability to engage readers with evocative narrative, realistic characters, and astute societal observations cemented her place as a key figure in contemporary crime fiction. Her early career not only established her as a successful author, but also lay the groundwork for a long and illustrious literary career.

CHAPTER 2

LITERARY WORK

LITERARY CAREER

Donna Leon's writing career spans more than three decades, during which time she has become one of the most recognized and respected figures in contemporary mystery fiction. In my response, I will go deeply into Donna Leon's literary career, examining the progression of her writing, the fundamental themes in her work, and her enduring popularity with readers all around the world.

Leon's writing career took off in 1992, when her debut novel, "Death at La Fenice," was published. The first book in the Commissario Guido Brunetti series introduced readers to the popular detective and the gorgeous setting of Venice. "Death at La Fenice" received critical acclaim almost immediately for its atmospheric representation of the city, interesting characters, and complicated storyline. The popularity of the novel laid the groundwork for Leon's continuous literary quest.

Leon has dazzled readers with a new installment of the Commissario Brunetti series practically every year since her debut. Over 30 volumes in the series have captivated audiences with their deep character development, intellectual storylines, and investigation of contemporary concerns. Leon addresses issues like as corruption, environmental degradation, immigration, and the challenges of current Italian culture through the perspective of crime fiction.

Leon's writing style is distinguished by vivid descriptions, painstaking attention to detail, and an acute knowledge of the human condition. She expertly combines sophisticated narratives, thought-provoking social criticism, and the distinct atmosphere of Venice to produce engaging and engrossing reading experiences. Her ability to capture the essence of the city's sights, sounds, and cultural nuances lends a real element to her storytelling.

One distinguishing feature of Leon's literary work is her dedication to keeping a constant and recognizable narrative voice. The Commissario Brunetti series has a consistency of style and character development, allowing readers to travel with the detective as he navigates the complexity of both Venice and his own personal life. Leon's deft characterizations help readers to identify with Brunetti's bright and sympathetic personality, forming a strong bond with the protagonist over the course of several chapters.

Aside from the Commissario Brunetti series, Donna Leon's writing career has taken her beyond criminal fiction. She has written independent novels such as "The Jewels of Paradise" and "The Waters of Eternal Youth," demonstrating her writing ability. These stand-alone works provide readers with peeks into diverse worlds, demonstrating Leon's ability to attract audiences even when they are not part of her well-known series.

Leon's writing has won various honors during her career, including significant literary awards and translations into multiple languages. Her works have struck a chord with readers not just because of their captivating stories, but also because of their ability to negotiate thorny moral quandaries and shed light on modern situations. As a result, Donna Leon has a devoted global following of readers who eagerly await each new release.

Donna Leon's literary career has been distinguished by consistency, captivating storytelling, and thought-provoking social commentary. She has caught readers' minds through the Commissario Brunetti trilogy and her standalone novels, taking them to the lovely streets of Venice while questioning their views and stimulating critical investigation of the society we live in. Donna Leon's creative achievements have cemented her reputation as a master of crime fiction and a revered personality in the literary world.

CREATION OF THE COMMISSARIO GUIDO BRUNETTI SERIES

The Commissario Guido Brunetti series by Donna Leon is a popular collection of crime novels set in Venice, Italy. The series follows Commissario Guido Brunetti's life and investigations as a conscientious and bright police detective.

One of the series' most prominent features is its detailed depiction of Venice as a setting for the storylines. Donna Leon's profound love and understanding of the city shine through in her descriptions, which capture Venice's distinct spirit and beauty. Canals, small lanes, and ancient landmarks become vital components of the story, providing depth and authenticity.

Commissario Guido Brunetti is a complicated and relatable figure. He is a family man who is married to Paola and has two children. Brunetti is noted for his honesty, knowledge, and compassion, which frequently prompts him to confront the moral and ethical quandaries posed in the cases he investigates. He is not afraid to question authority or society standards, which makes him a fascinating protagonist.

Throughout the series, Donna Leon addresses a wide range of social and political problems, using crime as a lens to examine corruption, injustice, and the intricacies of modern society. Her writing explores issues such as environmental deterioration, political corruption, immigration, and the growing wealth disparity. These themes give the stories depth and relevance, lifting them above the level of simple crime fiction.

Her Commissario Guido Brunetti series has a devoted fan base that appreciates the combination of gripping mysteries, vividly portrayed characters, and the atmospheric location of Venice. The series now has almost 30 novels, each with a new and exciting case for Brunetti to solve.

The Commissario Guido Brunetti series is a riveting collection of crime books that not only entertain but also provide thought-provoking insights into modern situations. Whether you enjoy crime fiction or want to learn more about the unique world of Venice through literature, this series is well worth your time.

GUIDO BRUNETTI SERIES SUMMARY

The series began in 1992 with the release of "Death at La Fenice" and has since grown to include over 30 books.

Commissario Guido Brunetti is a highly intelligent and sympathetic Venetian police officer. He is noted for his honesty and ability to manage Venice's complex social and political landscape. Brunetti is frequently confronted with cases that show the city's darker side, such as corruption, organized crime, and socioeconomic difficulties.

Brunetti is followed in each book in the series as he investigates a new crime, often involving murder. While the riddles are at the heart of the plot, Donna Leon's writing also digs into Venice's rich cultural and historical features. With its distinct atmosphere and obstacles, the city itself becomes a character in the series.

One of the most noticeable characteristics of the Commissario Guido Brunetti series is the emphasis on character development. Brunetti's personal life is examined throughout the volumes, including his relationship with his wife Paola and their children. This gives dimension to the narrative and allows readers to connect with the protagonist on a more personal level.

Donna Leon's writing style is frequently lauded for its evocative descriptions and astute societal analysis. She addresses a variety of subjects, including environmental concerns, governmental corruption, and the wealth gap. Leon's storytelling offers readers a thought-provoking and immersive experience.

While the books can be read as independent novels, the series has a chronological chronology, and recurring characters and storylines evolve over time. However, each novel can be enjoyed on its own.

CRITICAL RECEPTIONS AND POPULARITY

Donna Leon's Commissario Guido Brunetti series is well-known in the crime fiction community. The series is set in Venice, Italy, and follows Commissario Guido Brunetti, a thoughtful and morally oriented police detective. Brunetti's character, as well as Venice's atmospheric surroundings, have been lauded for their authenticity and depth.

Leon's superb storytelling, well-developed characters, and sophisticated plots have earned the series a devoted following of readers. Many readers like Leon's exploration of social and political topics in the context of a crime thriller, which provides a sophisticated and thought-provoking reading experience.

In terms of critical response, both readers and critics have given the Commissario Guido Brunetti series high marks. Leon's ability to blend gripping mysteries with astute societal commentary has received widespread acclaim. Her writing style, attention to detail, and ability to convey Venice's soul have all been praised.

The series' success can be observed in its longevity and the number of novels published. Donna Leon has authored nearly 30 novels featuring Commissario Guido Brunetti, demonstrating the character's and the series' lasting appeal. While the majority of her books are part of the Commissario Brunetti series, she has written a few solo novels as well.

DONNA STANDALONE NOVELS

"The Jewels of Paradise," one of Donna Leon's standalone novels, was published in 2012. Caterina Pellegrini, a musicologist, is engaged to analyse the contents of two trunks belonging to a Venetian family in this book. She discovers a mystery regarding a lost opera and a buried treasure as she delves into the family's history.

"The Girl of His Dreams," another standalone novel by Donna Leon, was published in 2008. Commissario Brunetti investigates the death of a young girl found in a Venetian canal in this book. He discovers a dark world of child trafficking and exploitation as he dives deeper.

Donna Leon's "The Waters of Eternal Youth" is yet another standalone novel, published in 2016. Commissario Brunetti analyses the story of a woman who fell into a canal as a youngster and has been mentally ill ever since in this novel. He discovers secrets and corruption inside the hospital system as he investigates the tragedy.

These are only a few of Donna Leon's standalone novels. Each book has its own story to tell and may be read separately of the Commissario Brunetti series. It is worth mentioning, however, that the majority of Donna Leon's admirers are drawn to the series' ongoing character development and repeating themes.

AN OVERVIEW OF DONNA STANDALONE NOVELS

➤ The Jewels of Paradise (2012)

Caterina Pellegrini, a musicologist, is engaged to evaluate the contents of two trunks belonging to a Venetian family in this tale. As she investigates the family's history, she discovers a mystery regarding a lost opera and a buried treasure.

➤ The Girl of His Dreams (2008)

In this novel, Commissario Brunetti investigates the death of a little girl found in a Venetian canal. As he dives deeper, he discovers a dark world of child trafficking and exploitation.

➤ The Waters of Eternal Youth (2016)

Commissario Brunetti investigates the case of a woman who fell into a canal as a youngster and has been psychologically damaged since. As he investigates the tragic events, he discovers secrets and corruption inside the healthcare system.

➤ The Temptation of Forgiveness (2018)

This novel examines the situation of a man who served time in prison for a violent crime yet claims to have changed. Commissario Brunetti is tasked with establishing if the individual is actually changed or if he continues to constitute a threat to society.

> ### Unto Us a Son Is Given (2019)

Commissario Brunetti investigates the odd circumstances surrounding the adoption of a young man by an elderly count in this book. As he investigates the family's history, he discovers hidden intentions and long-held secrets.

Through Donna Leon's compelling storytelling, these separate novels allow readers to discover different facets of Venice and its civilization. While these novels can be appreciated on their own, fans of Donna Leon's Commissario Brunetti series may find them interesting as they exhibit Donna Leon's expertise in constructing engaging mysteries and examining complicated societal themes.

DISTINCTIVE CHARACTERISTICS

Featuring her main character, Commissario Guido Brunetti, her distinct writing style and features have made her a well-known and acclaimed author in the crime fiction genre.

Donna Leon's work is noteworthy for its attention to detail and evocative descriptions of the city of Venice. She brings the city to life through her atmospheric and evocative prose, capturing the beauty, history, and unique charm of Venice. Her expertise and love of the city are clear in her writing, and she frequently utilizes it as a backdrop to explore diverse social, cultural, and political themes.

Donna Leon's novels are also distinguished by their rich and well-developed characters. The protagonist of the series, Commissario Guido Brunetti, is a serious and introspective detective who frequently finds himself navigating the moral complexity of the crimes he examines. Brunetti is a likable and sympathetic figure who draws readers in with his brilliance, ethics, and compassion. Leon also casts a large number of supporting characters, including Brunetti's family, colleagues, and friends, who bring depth and realism to her narrative.

Donna Leon's novels frequently deal with social and political topics, shedding light on corruption, injustice, and power abuse. She investigates subjects such as environmental degradation, illegal immigration, organized crime, and governmental corruption through the lens of her crime schemes. Leon's novels are not only about solving crimes; they are also a commentary of Italy's defects and injustices.

Furthermore, Donna Leon's writings frequently deal with ethical quandaries and moral complexity. Her stories are about more than just finding the bad guy; they also explore the grey regions between right and wrong. She poses provocative concerns about justice, morality, and the intricacies of human behavior. Leon's work urges readers to ponder on these topics and consider the broader consequences of the crimes and investigations depicted in her novels.

In summary, Donna Leon's distinct features as an author are her evocative descriptions of Venice, her well-developed and relatable characters, and her examination of social, political, and ethical concerns. Her crime novels go beyond mere entertainment, providing readers with a better grasp of the complexity of human nature and society.

COMPARING COMMISSARIO GUIDO BRUNETTI AND OTHER STANDALONE

Crime books by Donna Leon are gathered in the Commissario Guido Brunetti series. The series is set in Venice, Italy, and follows Commissario Guido Brunetti's investigations. Brunetti's quest to uncover a particular crime or mystery is the subject of each book in the series.

The recurrent characters and their evolution are one of the key contrasts between the Commissario Guido Brunetti series and solo novels. Readers get to know Brunetti and his family, as well as his colleagues and acquaintances, via the series. This enables them to delve deeper into their personalities, relationships, and personal lives. Standalone books, on the other hand, frequently introduce new characters with each volume, allowing for less long-term character development.

Another factor to consider is the environment. The series Commissario Guido Brunetti is well-known for its colorful and atmospheric descriptions of Venice. In the works, the city takes on the role of a character, and readers gain a sense of its own culture, history, and challenges. The setting of standalone novels may vary from book to book, and there may be less emphasis on immersing the reader in a single locale.

In terms of plot structure, each book in the Commissario Guido Brunetti series follows a similar formula. Typically, a crime or mystery is introduced at the start, Brunetti's investigation and eventual resolution follow. Standalone books, on the other hand, offer more story structure flexibility and can vary substantially in terms of pacing, twists, and turns.

It's worth mentioning that, while the Commissario Guido Brunetti series can be read in any order, there is some continuity in terms of character development and relationships. Standalone novels, on the other hand, can be read without any prior information or background.

Finally, the Commissario Guido Brunetti series allows readers to see Venice through the eyes of a seasoned detective. The recurrent characters and environment offer a sense of familiarity and continuity across the series. Standalone novels, on the other hand, provide more variety in terms of characters, places, and plot patterns. Both formats have advantages and disadvantages and can provide delightful reading experiences.

LITERARY WORKS IN GENERAL

Donna Leon's creative works range from mysteries and crime novels to historical fiction and essays.

Leon's most well-known series is on the character of Commissario Guido Brunetti, a pragmatic and introspective detective who investigates crimes on the streets of Venice. The Brunetti series is praised for its immersive storytelling and exciting plot twists that keep the reader engaged until the very end.

In addition to her crime fiction series, Leon has authored other single literary pieces that explore various themes and genres. For instance, She confronts the problem of healthcare privatization in "The Worst Intentions," while in "The Jewels of Paradise," she combines themes of mystery and history with classical music.

Leon's ability to catch the essence of Venice and portray it clearly and authentically is a distinguishing feature of her work. Her descriptions of Venice's canals, squares, and old buildings immerse the reader in the city's distinct ambiance, transforming it into a character in its own right.

Leon also uses her novels as a platform to investigate and question social and cultural issues. Her publications address a variety of themes, including political corruption, bureaucracy, immigration, and gender injustice. Leon delivers a realistic and occasionally critical representation of Italian and Western society in general through her characters and plots.

The NERO Wolfe Prize and the Corine Literature Prize are just a couple of the honors and distinctions Donna Leon has received during the course of her creative career. Her writings have been translated into various languages and have received widespread acclaim in Italy and around the world.

In a nutshell Donna Leon's literary works stand out for their ability to blend mystery and intrigue with acute social awareness and a genuine depiction of Venice. Her works immerse the reader in the city and handle pertinent issues from a distinct perspective.

POPULAR NOVELS

Donna Leon most famous series features Commissario Guido Brunetti, a detective in the Venetian police force. However, here are a few of her highly regarded novels:

➤ Death at La Fenice (1992)

This is the first novel in the Commissario Brunetti series, and it introduces readers to the detective and his investigations. The plot centers around the murder of a prominent conductor during a performance at the historic La Fenice opera theatre.

➢ **Acqua Alta (1996)**

Brunetti investigates the death of a museum director whose body is discovered in the flooded basement of his museum during the high tide known as "acqua alta." Brunetti is drawn into the world of art fraud and corruption as a result of his inquiry.

➢ **Uniform Justice (2003)**

Brunetti is dealing with a case involving the death of a young student at a famous military academy. As he digs deeper into the investigation, he discovers a network of secrets and a system that protects the privileged.

➢ **By Its Cover (2014)**

This novel is about the theft of rare books from a prominent library in Venice. Brunetti must negotiate the world of rare books and literary theft to solve the case.

➢ **Earthly Remains (2017)**

In this installment, Brunetti takes a leave of absence and escapes to a lonely island in the Venetian lagoon. Brunetti's pleasant vacation is disrupted when the caretaker of the villa where he is staying goes missing, and he becomes embroiled in a mystery disappearance.

DONNA LEON BIO

CHAPTER 3

UNIQUE WRITING STYLE

L eon is famous for her unusual writing style as well as the issues she covers in her works. Her attention to detail, atmospheric descriptions, and strong feeling of place distinguish her writing approach. Through her descriptive words, she provides a realistic picture of Venice, the city in which her novels are situated.

Leon's writing is frequently regarded as lyrical and poetic, with an emphasis on providing the reader with a sensory experience. She focuses on the sights, sounds, and fragrances of Venice, immersing the reader in the city's distinct ambiance. Her descriptions of Venice's canals, passageways, and old structures are rich and engaging, taking the reader to this lovely and mysterious city.

WRITING STYLE AND THEMES

Her writing style is distinguished by descriptive prose, meticulous attention to detail, and atmospheric locations. She has a talent for producing vivid and evocative environments, especially in her portrayal of Venice. Readers can virtually feel the dampness of the canals, hear the echoing footfall on the cobblestone streets, and smell the scent of espresso drifting from the cafes thanks to her evocative descriptions.

Leon's writing is especially notable for its exquisiteness and subtlety. She doesn't rely on spectacular action sequences or dramatic story twists to keep her readers interested. Instead, she focuses on the gradual unraveling of riddles, allowing suspense to grow over time. Her works are frequently more character-driven

25

than plot-driven, with a significant emphasis on her heroes' personal problems and motives.

One of Leon's frequent topics is corruption, both within the Italian government and the justice system. She exposes the ubiquitous impact of bribery, nepotism, and political maneuvering through her protagonist, Commissario Guido Brunetti. Brunetti's investigations frequently lead him to confront powerful persons who exploit the system for personal advantage, emphasizing the difficulties that those seeking justice face in a corrupt society.

She explores themes of inequality and social injustice in addition to corruption. She investigates topics such as class imbalance, immigrant discrimination, and the mistreatment of marginalized people. She illuminates the problems of those on the periphery of society through her storytelling and invites readers to evaluate their own preconceptions and biases.

Another common issue in Leon's works is the degradation of the environment. She utilizes her novels to spread awareness about the effects of pollution and climate change on Venice. She emphasizes the critical need for sustainable practices and environmental stewardship through her descriptions of rising sea levels, deteriorating structures, and dirty canals.

Leon writes about the intricacies of human relationships and emotions. Her characters are frequently flawed and multi-dimensional, dealing with emotional conflicts and moral quandaries. She delves into themes of loyalty, betrayal, love, and grief, weaving a complex tapestry of human experiences that readers will recognize.

Donna Leon's writing style is distinguished by descriptive descriptions, subtle storytelling, and study of social and environmental issues. She not only entertains readers with her fascinating narratives, but she also challenges them to reflect on the world around them and strive for a more just and sustainable society.

NARRATIVE TECHNIQUES

Donna Leon's narrative method is distinguished by its attention to detail, sensitivity, and slow pace. She has a talent for immersing readers in her novels' rich landscapes and atmospheric locales, particularly in her vivid representation of Venice. She provides a visceral experience for readers with her descriptive words, allowing them to practically feel, hear, and smell the metropolis she brings to life.

One of the most important characteristics of Leon's narrative method is her emphasis on the gradual unraveling of mysteries. She uses a more measured approach, allowing the suspense to grow gradually, rather than depending on spectacular action sequences or dramatic story twists. This helps readers to become totally immersed in her protagonist, Commissario Guido Brunetti's, investigation. Leon establishes a sense of reality and authenticity in her storytelling by delving into the complexities of the case.

Leon's stories are frequently character-driven rather than plot-driven. She goes deeply into her heroes' personal problems and motivations, presenting readers with a complex grasp of their thoughts and feelings. This allows viewers to feel more connected to the characters as they struggle with personal issues and moral quandaries. Leon's investigation of human connections and emotions gives her works depth and complexity, allowing them to connect with readers on a deeper level.

Leon's investigation of social and environmental issues is another noteworthy part of her narrative method. She uses her novels as a platform to expose corruption in the Italian government and legal system, exposing the difficulties that those seeking justice confront in a corrupt country. She also discusses issues of inequality, discrimination, and environmental damage. She raises awareness about these urgent topics through her novels and urges readers to reflect on their own preconceptions and biases.

Leon's writing also has a sense of depth and refinement. She doesn't tell readers everything, but rather gives opportunity for interpretation and investigation. This enables readers to connect with the material more deeply, reaching their own conclusions and reflecting on the themes and messages given in her works.

Donna Leon's narrative method is distinguished by its attention to detail, subtlety, and examination of social and environmental issues. She writes compelling narratives that not only entertain but also challenge readers to reflect on the world around them through her descriptive prose, subtle storytelling, and emphasis on character development.

In addition to her expert depiction of Venice, Leon's writing explores a variety of challenging concepts. The investigation of corruption and moral deterioration in society is a constant theme in her writings. Leon throws a light on Venice's dark underbelly, highlighting the corruption and deceit that exist beneath its picturesque veneer, through her protagonist, Commissario Guido Brunetti.

The investigation of social concerns and cultural critique is another important element in Leon's works. She uses her novels to promote awareness and spark debate on issues like as immigration, environmental degradation, and governmental corruption. Leon's stories frequently challenge cultural standards and put the current quo into question, encouraging readers to think critically about the world around them.

Leon's writing is also noted for its outstanding characterization. Her characters are multi-dimensional and complicated each with their own flaws, motivations, and backstories. She delves into her characters' inner life, digging into their thoughts and feelings to create empathy and understanding. This level of personality enriches and deepens her stories, allowing them to connect with readers on a deeper level.

The attention to detail, atmospheric descriptions, and strong sense of place distinguish Donna Leon's writing style. Her works deal with subjects such as corruption, social difficulties, and cultural commentary, as well as the complexity of human nature. Leon has established herself as a master of crime fiction and a powerful voice in contemporary literature due to her distinct writing style and thought-provoking issues.

WRITING DETECTIVE FICTION

Donna Leon is notable for her renowned series of detective books set in Venice, Italy. Her main character is Commissario Guido Brunetti, a police detective who solves crimes in the city.

Her writing style is frequently complimented for its attention to detail and vivid depictions of Venice. She expertly catches the soul of the city, its culture, and its people, adding depth and authenticity to her stories. Her detailed descriptions of the city's icons, canals, and hidden corners create a powerful sense of place, making readers feel as if they are right there in Venice.

Donna Leon's detective fiction is known for its attention on social and political themes. She addresses different subjects in her novels, including corruption, environmental problems, immigration, and the impact of globalization on traditional Venetian life. She uses her novels as a platform to bring these topics to light, frequently raising crucial questions and inspiring thinking in her readers.

The protagonist of Leon's works, Commissario Guido Brunetti, is a multifaceted and relatable figure. He is a committed and knowledgeable detective who is not hesitant to question authority or society standards. Brunetti's investigations frequently delve into Venice's dark underbelly, exposing corruption and moral quandaries inside the city's institutions.

Her novels are recognized for their slow-burning pace and sophisticated narrative. Her novels are about more than just solving murders; they are also about understanding the human condition and the complexity of relationships. She goes into the psyche of her characters, giving readers a better understanding of their motivations and actions.

In addition to fascinating storytelling, Leon's novel provide readers with an insight into Venice's rich culinary culture. Brunetti frequently enjoys great meals and discusses recipes with his wife, Paola, in her books. This adds a delicious and mouth-watering touch to the narrative.

In general, Donna Leon's detective fiction is praised for its atmospheric setting, intriguing issues, effective characters, and sophisticated plots. Her stories immerse readers in an immersive experience, transporting them to the gorgeous city of Venice while immersing them in intriguing mysteries.

VENICE AS A CENTRAL LOCATION

Donna Leon's novels are celebrated for their ability to capture the essence of Venice, taking readers to the lovely city and immersing them in its distinct ambiance. Leon brings the streets, canals, and landmarks of Venice to life with her vivid descriptions and attention to detail, allowing readers to experience the city's beauty and charm.

Her deep understanding and affection for Venice is one of the essential characteristics of Leon's writing that contributes to a genuine picture of the city. Leon has lived in Venice for almost thirty years and has a thorough awareness of its history, tradition, and social structure. This personal knowledge of the city shines through in her stories, as she deftly weaves in information about its architecture, art, foods, and cultures.

Leon's depiction of Venice extends beyond its lovely facade. She delves into the city's complicated social and political scene, examining the clashes between old and new, tradition and modernization. Leon navigates the complicated web of Venetian society through her protagonist, Commissario Guido Brunetti, exposing its hidden secrets and putting light on the darker parts that lurk under the surface.

Venice becomes more than a backdrop in Leon's writings; it becomes a character in its own right. The canals, bridges, and small lanes of the city become important to the plot, bringing a feeling of place and complexity to the narrative. Leon's attention to detail shines through in her descriptions of the city's architecture, from the magnificence of St. Mark's Square to the crumbling façade of lesser-known neighborhoods. These descriptions not only produce a vivid picture, but also inspire a sense of unchanging history.

31

Leon's works also depict the particular rhythm of life in Venice. She depicts the daily routines and rituals that characterize the life of Venetians, from hectic marketplaces to peaceful moments of contemplation by the river. She addresses the problems and joys of living in a city that is both a tourist destination and a close-knit community through her characters.

Finally, Donna Leon's novels are excellent at portraying the essence of Venice. Her thorough knowledge of the city brings its streets, waterways, and monuments to life, producing an engaging reading experience. Her attention to detail, examination of social relationships, and depiction of daily life in Venice all contribute to the novels' realism. Donna Leon's works are an excellent alternative for those looking for a thrilling voyage into the heart of Venice.

VENICE: THE CHARACTER

Donna Leon's crime fiction novels are mostly set in Venice, and the city plays an important role in her works. Her descriptive descriptions of the city and its culture immerse readers in the distinctive characteristics of Venice, examining the city's rich history, art, and architecture.

Leon's superb portrayals of Venice allow readers to enjoy the city's splendor while also learning about its underlying difficulties. The city's diverse neighborhoods, winding canals, and great architecture serve as the ideal setting for her enthralling narratives, leaving readers in awe and intrigue. Her attention to detail is impeccable, and her descriptions of the city transport you into its streets.

Her works center on Venice's cultural components, emphasizing its conventions, traditions, and rituals. She investigates Venetian

32

culture, frequently focusing on the city's complicated ties and social dynamics. She also goes deeper into the city's political and economic concerns, providing insight into contemporary themes such as corruption, bureaucracy, and gentrification.

One of Leon's most amazing qualities is how she employs Venice as a character in her stories. Venice is brought to life in her paintings, with the city becoming a character in the narrative she recounts. The city's monuments, such as the Rialto Bridge and Saint Mark's Basilica, play an important role in the plot of her works, serving as a navigational reference point for the reader.

Leon's descriptions of Venice immerse readers in the story, allowing them to get immersed in it. The city's wealth and complexity create a setting steeped in history and charm. The city, with its small alleys, arched bridges, and peculiar canals, provides a unique background for her works, and Venice frequently takes on a life of its own in her novels.

One of Donna Leon's greatest qualities is her description of Venice as a crucial backdrop. The city is skillfully intertwined into her pieces, becoming a character in its own right. Her authentic and intricate descriptions of Venice provide readers with a deeper knowledge of the city's culture, history, and architecture, giving a complex and captivating backdrop. Venetians frequently claim that their city is a book that must be reread in order to be fully comprehended. Donna Leon's works are an important part of the Venetian literary environment, contributing to the riveting story of a city that never ceases to amaze.

EXPLORATION OF MUSIC AND OPERA

Music is frequently a major element in Donna Leon's writings, and she uses it to heighten the mood and give readers a better understanding of the characters' thoughts and feelings. Commissario Brunetti is a fan of classical music, particularly opera, and his love of music is a constant theme throughout the series.

She addresses music and opera in her novels through the figure of Commissario Brunetti's wife, Paola. Paola is an English literature professor who loves opera. She frequently discusses and introduces Brunetti to numerous operas, composers, and performers, establishing a link between the characters and the world of music.

Donna Leon explores the deep history and significant cultural impact of opera under the influence of Paola. She investigates many operas, their stories, and the feelings they arouse. The author also discusses the difficulties faced by performers, the commitment needed to put on a production, and the inner workings of opera houses.

Readers can completely engross themselves in the world of sound and melody thanks to Donna Leon's vivid and thorough descriptions of music and opera. She effectively conveys the ability of music to elicit feelings, carry listeners to many locations and eras, and offer comfort and an escape from the harsh truths of life.

In addition, Donna Leon employs opera and music in her books to examine social and political themes. She often incorporates real-life events and controversies from the world of music, shedding light on the darker aspects of the industry. Through her storytelling, she raises questions about power, corruption, and the exploitation of artists.

To sum up, Donna Leon's novels have a richer, deeper quality because of the way she explores opera and music in her writing. She explores the emotional and cultural relevance of music by focusing on Commissario Brunetti and his wife Paola. She does this by utilizing music as a tool to improve the mood, create characters, and address more general social themes.

CHAPTER 4

ICONIC WRITING PROCESS

Donna Leon's writing process is frequently brought up in interviews and chats. We can learn how she approaches her profession and generates engaging stories that have captivated people all across the world by reading her remarks.

Rigorous research is one component of her writing technique that stands out. She believes in immersing herself in her novels' settings, which are primarily situated in Venice. She spends a large amount of time in the city, observing daily life, conversing with residents, and discovering hidden gems. This attention to detail enables her to portray Venice in her writings in a realistic and vivid manner.

Donna Leon has stated in interviews that she frequently begins her novels with an idea or a theme that she wishes to explore. This could be a social issue, a moral quandary, or an examination of human nature. She then builds her plot and characters around this primary notion, constructing a gripping story that keeps readers interested.

Her writing is noted for its deep feeling of place. She has stated that the city of Venice is a character in her stories, and she works hard to convey its distinct mood and culture. We can tell from her comments that she regards Venice as a source of inspiration and a setting that gives complexity and richness to her works.

Another fascinating feature of Leon's process of writing is her approach to character development. In interviews, she has stated that she enjoys creating characters who are complicated and multi-dimensional, with flaws and strengths that make them sympathetic to readers. She believes that characters should grow and evolve throughout the course of a series, and she enjoys exploring their inner travels and relationships.

She has also discussed the significance of pacing in her writings. She believes in driving the plot ahead while maintaining a balance of suspense and character development. She wants her readers to feel involved and invested in the plot, as well as get to know the characters on a more personal level.

Donna Leon's writing technique is distinguished by rigorous research, a strong feeling of place, and an emphasis on developing unique and accessible characters. We may learn a lot about how she approaches her profession and brings her stories to life from her comments in interviews and chats. More information is provided below.

PROCESS OF WRITING

Donna Leon's writing method is precise and thoughtful, reflecting her commitment to creating engaging crime thrillers set in Venice. While she hasn't disclosed many specifics about her method, there are certain insights from interviews and her own remarks that offer light on her approach to writing.

Leon spends a significant amount of time researching before she begins writing. This study covers a broad range of subjects, including art, history, cultural nuances, Italian politics, and social issues. She feels that a thorough understanding of the setting in which her stories take place is essential for creating an authentic and engaging reading experience.

Leon does not plan out her works in great detail before beginning to write. Instead, she lets the plot unfold naturally as she goes. This approach allows for spontaneity and allows her characters to develop spontaneously within the context of the plot. In interviews, she has stated that the characters occasionally surprise her with their decisions, sending the plot in unexpected areas.

Venice is central to Leon's works, and she considers the city to be one of her characters. She describes Venice as a real, breathing creature that shapes her characters' behavior and thoughts. Leon spends a large amount of time in Venice, taking in the sights, sounds, and ambiance, to assure accuracy and portray the soul of the city. Immersion in the area allows her to weave vivid descriptions and authentic details into her work, bringing Venice to life on the page.

Leon's literary style stands out for its compassion, precise wording, and meticulous attention to detail. She believes it is critical to allow the reader to actively engage with the material, drawing their own conclusions and filling in gaps. Her style has been regarded as exquisite and evocative, and she writes at a slow, deliberate pace that allows readers to savor the nuances of her tale.

The editing process is an important aspect of Leon's writing process. She goes over and revises her draughts thoroughly, giving close attention to language, structure, and character development. She has stated that she frequently rewrites extensively, revising until she is satisfied with the final product. This drive to improve her work contributes to her novels' polished and well-crafted quality.

In terms of her writing routine, Leon prefers to write in the mornings when her mind is fresh. She has mentioned that she aims for a quota of a certain number of pages per day, as this helps her maintain a sense of progress and momentum in her writing. However, she also allows for flexibility and acknowledges that some days can be more productive than others.

Donna Leon's writing process is characterized by meticulous research, a flexible approach to plot development, a deep connection to the setting of Venice, careful editing, and an elegant literary style. This combination of factors contributes to the distinct and captivating nature of her crime novels, creating a reading experience that is both immersive and thought-provoking.

INSPIRATION AND RESEARCH

To build the rich and authentic worlds described in her works, Donna Leon draws inspiration from a range of sources and does thorough study. Her dedication to rigorous research is evident in the precise descriptions of Venetian life, cultural nuances, historical context, and political environment that pervade her writings.

One of Leon's key sources of inspiration is her strong affection and connection to Venice. Leon has lived in the city for over 30 years and has gained a deep understanding and admiration for its distinct atmosphere, labyrinthine canals, and rich history. Venice is an important character in her stories, with its beauty and secrets frequently serving as a backdrop for the unfolding mysteries. Leon's love of and knowledge of Venice infuses her writing with a genuine sense of place, allowing readers to experience the city's charm and intricacies.

Leon's observations and experiences in Italy also contribute to her inspiration. She maintains an outsider's perspective as an expat living in Italy, providing her with a new prism through which to see the complexities of Italian society and culture. Her excellent eye for detail and ability to depict subtle social interactions are aided by her foreigner's perspective on navigating and interpreting Italian life. This viewpoint enables her to dive into the unique quirks of Italian society and study its strengths, challenges, and inconsistencies.

Leon's writing method includes extensive research. She spends a significant amount of time conducting detailed study before beginning a new work. Her dedication to accuracy and authenticity motivates her to research a wide range of topics. She investigates art, history, music, literature, culinary traditions, political concerns, local customs, and other topics through her research. This comprehensive investigation guarantees that her narratives are founded on solid knowledge, allowing her to masterfully create rich storylines that resonate with readers.

Her research also includes interviews with specialists from many sectors. She conducts interviews with people from various backgrounds, such as art historians, attorneys, musicians, and cultural specialists, to gain insights and assure factual correctness. These encounters with locals and professionals offer her with vital perspectives and enable her to weave the complexities of Venetian life and Italian society into her writing, strengthening the realism of her narratives.

Furthermore, Leon's works frequently address current and relevant social concerns. Leon does extensive study to ensure a clear understanding of these topics and their relation to the Italian setting. This research gives her the opportunity to shed light on issues such as corruption, racism, environmental problems, and the influence of organized crime. She develops narratives that engage and contribute to critical dialogues by basing her stories in real-world concerns.

Finally, Donna Leon is inspired by her personal connection to Venice, her outsider viewpoint on Italian society, and her dedication to careful research. Her strong passion for Venice infuses her writing with a genuine feeling of location, while her extensive research maintains the truth and authenticity of her narratives. Leon crafts engaging crime stories that not only entertain but also offer insights into the nuances of the Venetian and Italian worlds through her keen observations, conversations with specialists, and examination of social concerns.

INFLUENCES AND LITERARY REFERENCES

Donna Leon's work is influenced by a wide range of literary references and influences, which contribute to the depth and sophistication of her crime thrillers. Her writing demonstrates a great understanding of literary traditions, incorporates elements of classical literature, and draws inspiration from a wide range of authors and genres.

The tradition of crime fiction itself has had a significant influence on Leon's writing. She draws inspiration from the works of authors such as Agatha Christie, Arthur Conan Doyle, and Georges Simenon. Her writings demonstrate a great appreciation for the structure, suspense, and puzzle-solving elements that constitute the crime fiction genre. However, Leon's writing transcends standard crime fiction tropes by combining complicated riddles with social commentary and cultural research.

Classical literature is also a significant impact on Leon. She has mentioned Shakespeare's impact on her writing, stating that his ability to depict human complexity and moral difficulties has left a lasting impression on her. These influences can be observed in her works' rich characters and ethical dilemmas. Furthermore, Leon frequently inserts literary references inside her novels, giving perceptive connections that enrich the thematic complexity of her storytelling.

In Leon's writings, Venice itself becomes a literary influence. Her novels are set against the backdrop of Venice's rich literary heritage, which includes renowned individuals such as Shakespeare, Byron, and Thomas Mann. Leon skillfully weaves these literary references into her narratives, enhancing the sense of place and drawing on the city's cultural legacy.

Leon's interest in Italian literature can also be seen in her works. She admires authors like Italo Calvino, Elsa Morante, and Primo Levi, whose works explore Italian society, history, and identity. Leon's investigation of social and political themes within the context of her crime narratives bears witness to their effect. Leon develops multi-layered novels that go beyond basic entertainment, addressing deep topics and societal concerns by fusing crime fiction with elements of Italian literature.

Furthermore, Leon's interests and literary references are heavily influenced by music. She has a profound love of classical music and frequently includes references to composers and works in her novels. Music takes on a symbolic role, offering emotional resonance as well as a thematic underpinning. Her writing's evocative quality is enhanced by the intricate linkages between music, atmosphere, and character development.

Donna Leon's literary references and influences are numerous and deep. Her writing is influenced by crime fiction traditions, historical literature, Venice's rich literary heritage, Italian literature, and music. Leon develops storylines that go beyond the bounds of the crime fiction genre, diving into social issues, cultural study, and philosophical questions. Her deft use of literary allusions adds depth and complexity to her stories, giving readers an immersive and intellectually interesting reading experience.

CHALLENGES AND REWARD OF WRITING

Donna Leon, like many other writers, faces both problems and benefits as she pursues her literary career. The process of writing and revising novels has its own set of challenges, but it also provides immense personal fulfillment and the potential to connect with readers on a deep level.

One of Leon's concerns is keeping the creativity and inspiration required for her work. Writing a crime fiction necessitates the development of sophisticated plots, the creation of interesting characters, and the weaving together of engaging narratives. This creative process can be taxing and mentally draining, necessitating intense concentration and perseverance. Overcoming writer's block or discovering new approaches to storytelling can be an ongoing difficulty for any author, including Leon.

Another big challenge Leon confronts is the research required for her works. Her dedication to depth and authenticity necessitates extensive research into areas such as art, history, politics, and Venetian culture. Accurate information can be time-consuming and needs precise attention to detail. Leon must strike a delicate balance between ensuring that the details effortlessly merge with the plot and avoids dominating the narrative.

Furthermore, Leon faces the task of accurately portraying delicate social concerns. Her crime novels frequently address issues such as corruption and social justice. To address these subjects in a nuanced and courteous manner, extensive study, sensitivity, and a careful balancing act between entertainment and advocacy are required. Attempting to approach these themes with consideration and sensitivity complicates the writing process and necessitates a thorough awareness of the social and ethical implications at hand.

Despite the difficulties, Donna Leon finds great satisfaction in her work. The opportunity to construct and mold entire universes within her novels is one of the most significant rewards. Leon has the ability as a writer to create characters, elaborate mysteries, and transport readers to the vivid environment of Venice. Creating these universes allows her to share her imagination and point of view with readers, immersing them in thought-provoking stories.

Writing also gives Leon the chance to research and analyze issues pertaining to society. She can use her works to bring light on corruption, inequality, and other critical issues, stirring debate and boosting awareness among readers. Leon finds it extremely fulfilling to be able to use her writing platform to interact with critical issues and contribute to society discussion.

Furthermore, the author-reader interaction offers Leon a great deal of delight and fulfillment. Readers who identify with her characters, admire her narrative, and engage with the issues of her novels provide a substantial amount of satisfaction. Knowing that her works connect with readers and have a lasting impact on their lives is a reward that fuels her desire to write.

In closing, in her crime novels, Donna Leon faces problems associated with the creative process, research requirements, and the obligation of addressing societal issues. However, the benefits of writing, such as the capacity to build new worlds, investigate social concerns, and connect with readers, far outweigh the difficulties. Donna Leon finds her writing journey to be a highly fulfilling experience because of the personal fulfillment she derives from storytelling and the effect she can create with her narratives.

DONNA LEON BIO

CHAPTER 5

IMPACTS AND RECEPTION

CRITICAL RECEPTION

Reviewers and literary experts have praised Donna Leon's writing ability, character development, and evocative setting. Her works have received widespread acclaim for being fascinating and thought-provoking, with many critics praising the depth and intricacy of her narratives.

Leon's ability to build well-developed and relatable characters is one facet of her work that has gotten continuous praise. Commissario Guido Brunetti, the series' protagonist, has been praised for being an intriguing and multi-dimensional character. Critics like his depth of character, as well as his moral compass and brilliance. Brunetti's relationships with other characters, including his wife Paola and coworkers, have also been commended for their honesty and emotional impact.

In addition to her great character development, Leon's novels are widely praised for their rich and intricately knit narratives. Critics have noticed that her puzzles go beyond solving crimes to address wider social and political themes. In her stories, Leon addresses issues such as corruption, environmental destruction, and the wealth divide. This conceptual richness enriches her stories and takes them above the level of standard crime fiction.

Leon's ability to transport readers to Venice via atmospheric descriptions has also been greatly praised. Her colorful and evocative writing style, which brings the city to life on the paper, has been hailed by critics. Her commitment to detail in depicting

Venice's drainage channels, architecture, and culture produces an immersive and authentic feeling of location. Many people have said that reading Leon's works is like taking a trip to Venice.

Leon's contribution to the crime fiction genre cannot be emphasized. Her writings have been recognized for revitalizing the genre and providing it with a new viewpoint. Critics have highlighted that her emphasis on social themes and her examination of Italian society distinguishes her from other crime fiction authors. Leon's ability to blend exciting mysteries with social commentary has been credited with upgrading the genre and garnering a larger audience.

Her influence on Italian culture and literature has been extensively recognized outside of the literary sphere. Her works have received recognition for their penetrating depictions of Italian society and politics, as well as their explorations of corruption and moral quandaries. According to critics, Leon's art depicts Italy in a subtle and realistic manner, shedding light on both its beauty and its problems. Her works are regarded as significant contributions to current Italian writing, providing a distinct viewpoint on the country and its people.

Donna Leon's work has received overwhelmingly good critical response. Her writing ability, character development, evocative setting, and thematic depth have been commended by reviewers and literary critics. Her influence on the crime fiction genre and Italian writing in general has been highly acknowledged, with her novels being praised for their unique perspectives and perceptive societal commentary. Donna Leon's accomplishments have established her as a highly regarded and important writer in the literary world.

INFLUENCE ON THE GENRE OF CRIME FICTION

Donna Leon's contribution to the crime fiction genre cannot be overestimated. She has revitalized the genre and provided a new viewpoint to it with her distinctive style of narrative and study of societal concerns.

Leon's emphasis on social commentary has had a significant impact on crime fiction. While many crime novels focus on investigating crimes and apprehending offenders, Leon goes beyond this to address wider societal issues. She addresses issues like inequality between the rich and the poor, corruption, and environmental damage in her works. Leon elevates and broadens the genre by including these issues throughout her works. She demonstrates that crime fiction can be used for more than just amusement; it can also be used to explore major social and political topics.

Another facet of Leon's work that has had a big impact on the genre is her ability to construct well-developed and relatable characters. Commissario Guido Brunetti, her protagonist, is an engaging and multi-dimensional character who connects with readers. Brunetti is a likeable and interesting protagonist due to his moral compass, intelligence, and emotional depth. Leon goes above the traditional crime story template by focusing on character development. Other crime fiction authors have been encouraged by this emphasis on complex characters to pay closer attention to the psychological aspects of their characters, resulting in more nuanced and realistic portrayals.

In addition to her philosophical depth and great character development, Leon's evocative setting has had an impact on the crime fiction genre. Readers are transported to Venice through her descriptive and vivid descriptions, where they become engrossed in the city's distinctive ambiance. The city itself becomes a character in her novels, bringing another element of intrigue and depth to the storylines. This emphasis on setting has influenced other crime fiction writers to focus more on generating a sense of place in their stories. Leon brings richness and authenticity to her stories by bringing the location to life, making them more immersive and unforgettable.

Her influence on the crime fiction genre extends beyond her writing ability. Her ability to blend exciting mysteries with social commentary has brought the genre to a wider readership. Leon has made crime fiction more relevant and accessible to readers who may not have previously been interested in the genre by addressing major social themes in her stories. Her work has demonstrated that crime fiction can be academically fascinating and thought-provoking, drawing readers who seek more than a straightforward whodunit.

Leon's impact on the crime fiction genre extends beyond the literary realm. Her works have also had an enormous influence on Italian culture and literature. Leon illuminates both the beauty and imperfections of Italy through her astute description of Italian society and politics, as well as her examination of corruption and moral quandaries. Her work depicts the country in a subtle and realistic manner, helping to a better understanding of its people and culture. Leon's contribution to Italian literature has cemented his position as a major writer in both the crime fiction genre and the larger literary world.

Donna Leon has had a huge impact on the crime fiction genre. She has revitalized the genre and introduced a fresh viewpoint to it through her focus on social commentary, great character development, evocative setting, and ability to draw a wider audience. Her works provide vital insights into Italian society and politics, and her influence reaches beyond the literary world.

Donna Leon's accomplishments have left an unmistakable effect on crime fiction, confirming her position as a highly recognized and prominent writer in the genre.

TRANSLATIONS AND GLOBAL REACH

Donna Leon's novels have achieved widespread international acclaim and have been translated into other languages. Her works have been published in a number of countries, allowing readers worldwide to appreciate her stories.

Leon's ability to tell stories that resonate with a worldwide audience is one of the reasons for her international popularity. Her stories are set in Venice and frequently explore Italian society and culture, yet the topics she discusses are global. Issues like as corruption, justice, and morality are relevant to readers everywhere.

Translations of Leon's novels are critical to her international success. Publishers assist people who may not understand her language to enjoy her stories by making her works available in many languages. Translators are critical in capturing the essence of Leon's writing and effectively presenting it to readers in a variety of linguistic and cultural contexts.

It is worth mentioning that the quality of translations can have a significant impact on an author's international success. A great translation not only precisely translates the language but also captures the subtleties, tone, and style of the original work. This ensures that readers of different languages can completely understand Leon's storytelling.

Furthermore, publisher marketing and distribution activities contribute to Leon's works' international appeal. Publishers labor to promote her novels in various areas, making them available in retailers, online platforms, and libraries worldwide. This accessibility allows readers from all around the world to discover and participate in her works.

More so, the global popularity of crime fiction as a genre influences Leon's international reach. Crime fiction has a diverse readership spanning countries and languages, and Leon's brilliant narrative and captivating characters have drawn followers from many walks of life.

Finally, Donna Leon's novels have gained international acclaim through translations, allowing readers from all over the world to appreciate her stories. Her global popularity is due to the universal issues she tackles, the quality of translations, and the efforts of publishers.

TRANSLATIONS AND INTERNATIONAL RECOGNITION

Donna Leon's international acclaim and translations have helped to broaden her impact in the crime fiction genre. Her works have been translated into a number of languages, allowing readers all around the world to access and enjoy her work.

Leon's ability to convey the essence of Venice, Italy in her works is one of the primary aspects contributing to her international popularity. Her brilliant descriptions of the city's canals, architecture, and distinct ambiance have struck a chord with readers of all countries and origins. Because of her international appeal, her novels have been translated into a variety of languages, including Spanish, French, German, and Japanese. Through Leon's writing, readers all over the world have been able to experience the beauty and intrigue of Venice.

Her analysis of social themes, as well as her sensitive portrayal of Italian society, has also contributed to her international acclaim. Her books address global issues such as corruption, environmental degradation, and social unfairness, which resonate with readers all across the world. Leon provides a broader view on societal challenges that transcend national boundaries through her astute commentary on these concerns. Her work is highly sought after by publishers and readers all around the world because of its universal significance.

The translations of Leon's works have also contributed to her international recognition as a prominent writer in the crime fiction genre. Her distinct writing style, which incorporates social commentary and well-developed characters, has acquired a large readership outside of Italy. Leon has broadened the appeal of crime fiction and drawn in new readers by making her work available to readers in many languages. This has helped crime fiction as a whole gain ground and become more widespread, in addition to raising her profile internationally.

Donna Leon's international popularity can be credited to her various prizes and distinctions, in addition to her literary accomplishments. Her works have won critical acclaim and significant literary awards, including the CWA Macallan Silver Dagger for Fiction and the German Corine Literature Prize. These honors have increased awareness of Leon's work and reinforced her reputation as a highly renowned and influential writer.

Donna Leon's international acclaim and translations have helped to spread her influence in the crime fiction genre. Her ability to capture the essence of Venice, investigate critical social concerns, and develop believable people has endeared her to readers all over the world. Her work has reached audiences from all countries and backgrounds through translations, helping to the international expansion and appeal of crime fiction. Donna Leon's international acclaim attests to her writing talent and important contributions to the genre.

TELEVISION MODIFICATIONS

Donna Leon's acclaimed crime novel series starring Commissario Guido Brunetti has been successfully adapted for television, bringing her compelling stories and adored characters to life on the big screen. The television adaptations have gotten a lot of attention and appreciation, attracting both existing book readers and new viewers who are discovering Leon's work through television.

The first television version of a Donna Leon novel, "Vendetta," was released in 2000, directed by Christian von Castelberg. What would eventually turn into a profitable and long-running series was launched by this initial adaption. Since then, other novels from the Commissario Brunetti series have been adapted, providing lovers of the books a consistent and entertaining viewing experience.

The painstaking attention to capturing the essence of Donna Leon's Venice is one of the great triumphs of the television adaptations. The beautiful city, with its convoluted canals, old buildings, and distinct atmosphere, plays an important role in Leon's writings. The television adaptations have succeeded in recreating this distinct atmosphere, providing viewers with a visually rich and engaging experience. The famous pictures of Venice's landmarks, paired with the study of lesser-known locales, add to Leon's storytelling by enhancing the sense of place.

54

The representation of the principal character, Commissario Guido Brunetti, is critical to the success of the television versions. Brunetti is played by actor Uwe Kockisch, whose nuanced performance has been greatly lauded by fans and reviewers alike. Kockisch's portrayal of Brunetti catches the essence of the character, depicting a detective who is both brilliant and sensitive, while being endowed with compassion and a sense of justice. Kockisch's great acting has helped bring Brunetti to life, allowing viewers to empathize with the character's intricacies and moral quandaries.

The adaptations have been given depth and richness by also bringing to life supporting characters from the books. Julia Jäger, who plays Paola, Brunetti's wife, plays a crucial role in the show by highlighting their devoted and enduring relationship. Brunetti's contacts with his Questura coworkers—most particularly, those of Inspector Lorenzo Vianello, played by Karl Fischer, and Lieutenant Claudia Griffoni, played by Annett Renneberg—help to create the atmosphere of friendship and cooperation that is so important to the stories. These expertly constructed performances raise the quality of the adaptations overall and give them a strong ensemble cast that accurately represents the spirit of the source books.

The authenticity of the television adaptations to the original material is one of their significant advantages. In order to preserve the integrity and complexity of Donna Leon's plots, the screenwriters and directors frequently used her novels as the basis for the scripts. The positive response of the adaptations among devoted readers of the novels is probably due to this commitment to maintaining the spirit of the books.

The television adaptations have not only appealed to the books' devoted followers but also attracted new viewers who might not have previously read Donna Leon's works. The adaptations now have the ability to appeal to a wider audience because to the popularity and accessibility of criminal procedural dramas. The captivating plots, interesting mysteries, and endearing characters have drawn viewers in who may not have read the books, further solidifying Donna Leon's reputation as a brilliant storyteller.

Donna Leon's Commissario Brunetti series has been successfully adapted for television. Viewers have been immersed in the experience because to the cast's superb performances and the attention paid to accurately capture the essence of Venice. Both current fans and new audiences have expressed a strong interest in the adaptations thanks to their fidelity to the original material and expert handling of the complex themes. The television adaptations of Donna Leon's crime novels have increased the audience's understanding of her adored characters while highlighting Venice's attractiveness and Commissario Guido Brunetti's enduring appeal.

POPULAR APPEAL AND READERS RESPONSE

Over the years, a devoted fan base has grown up around Donna Leon's works due to their immense popularity. Her criminal novels, particularly the Commissario Guido Brunetti series, have become highly anticipated publications, with readers all around the world anxiously anticipating them. Several elements contribute to her enormous popularity and reader reactions to her books, including her fascinating storytelling, well-developed characters, immersive settings, and thought-provoking issues.

Donna Leon's ability to build engaging and sophisticated storylines is one of the key reasons for her popularity. Her novels are expertly constructed, bringing tension, mystery, and intrigue that keep readers hooked from start to finish. Leon's ability to weave together a complicated web of clues, motives, and red herrings provides a fascinating narrative that will appeal to crime fiction aficionados.

Leon's success is dependent on her development of the persona Commissario Guido Brunetti. Readers have become fond to Brunetti, finding him sympathetic, complex, and empathetic. Readers are drawn into Brunetti's universe and get concerned in his investigations because of his introspective character, passion to justice, and moral compass. Brunetti's personal life, including his relationship with his family and interactions with his coworkers, provides dimension to the stories and adds to the series' overall appeal.

Furthermore, Donna Leon's realistic depiction of Venice, Italy, provides as an enthralling backdrop for her works. The rich history, distinct culture, and stunning vistas of Venice are expertly represented, producing a sense of place that brings readers immediately into the heart of Venice. Leon's vivid descriptions and immersive writing style let readers to experience the city's beauty, charm, and gloom, which adds to the attractiveness of her writings.

Readers have been extremely complimentary about Donna Leon's novels. Fans like her ability to address current social and political themes within the context of a detective book. Leon deftly weaves subjects like corruption, environmental concerns, immigration, and the influence of tourism into her stories, presenting readers with a thought-provoking and nuanced viewpoint on these issues. Leon's novels encourage readers to consider the intricacies of society while still providing an amusing and engaging reading experience.

Donna Leon's books have also been lauded for their elegant prose and attention to detail. Her writing is distinguished by its elegance, wit, and refinement. Each sentence is well designed, allowing readers to savor the language and appreciate the creativity that goes into the storytelling. Leon's ability to stir emotions and create vivid imagery through her words has captured readers and gained her accolades from both reviewers and literary circles.

In addition to critical acclaim, Donna Leon's works have a devoted international following. Her books have been translated into a variety of languages, allowing people from all around the world to enjoy her stories. Fans can interact and share their love for her novels through online forums, book clubs, and social media platforms dedicated to discussing and analyzing her works.

The popularity of Donna Leon's books and readers' responses to them may be largely due to her adept storytelling, richly realized characters, vivid settings, and provocative issues. She has established herself as one of the most well-liked writers in the crime fiction genre thanks to her ability to enthrall readers with her complex plots, as well as her evocative writing style and social commentary.

CHAPTER 6

EXPLORATION OF SOCIAL ISSUES

SOCIAL ISSUES AND CULTURAL COMMENTARIES

For her crime fiction books set in Venice, Italy, Donna Leon is well known. She writes intriguing detective fiction as well as novels that offer perceptive analysis of contemporary social concerns and cultural commentary.

Corruption in Italian society is one of the major subjects she explores in her writing. She frequently exposes corruption in the Italian judicial, police, and government institutions in her works. The political corruption and mafia influence in the Italian justice system are depicted in Leon's novel "Death and Judgment," while in "Blood from a Stone," she exposes the widespread corruption in the local government's approval processes for new development. By stressing the inadequacies and flaws in its systems, she paints a gloomy image of Italy's social, political, and economic infrastructure.

The position of women in Italian society is a significant topic that is investigated. Despite residing in a contemporary culture, Leon deftly captures the constraints and difficulties Italian women endure. In Italy, women still experience discrimination, sexual harassment, and patriarchal standards that have an impact on their daily lives. In her piece "Death at La Fenice," Leon tackles this issue head-on by challenging the idea of sexually liberated and empowered Italian women and presenting a more complex and nuanced reality.

In addition to the aforementioned topics, Leon also discusses problems in her writings such as degradation of the environment, prejudice against immigrants, and police brutality. Her books offer a sharp critique of the problems and shortcomings of Italian society as well as a mirror for all of western civilization. Her writings are given a unique flavor by Leon's incredibly thorough descriptions of Venetian culture, which offer insights into the daily lives of city dwellers.

To sum up, Donna Leon does a remarkable job of incorporating social commentary and cultural themes into her works. Her books teach readers about the difficulties and complexities of Italian society in addition to engrossing them with suspenseful detective fiction. Her incisive stories provide readers the chance to think critically about current social concerns while becoming engrossed in the captivating and expertly written scenarios.

ETHICS AND MORALITY

Themes like corruption, justice, power, and the repercussions of one's actions are frequently discussed in Leon's writings. She poses concerns regarding the morality of people, institutions, and their effects on society. She investigates the moral decisions they make and the moral conundrums they encounter through the characters she creates.

The conflict between justice and the constraints of the judicial system is a recurrent issue in Leon's writings. Brunetti frequently runs into circumstances where the administration of justice is impeded by political influence, bureaucracy, or corruption. This raises concerns about the moral ramifications of those in positions of power and their ethical obligations.

The examination of societal difficulties is another part of ethics and morality in Leon's writings. She discusses issues such as environmental degradation, immigration, and social inequality, prompting readers to consider their own ethical principles and moral responsibilities to others.

It is crucial to recognize that reader' interpretations of ethics and morality in literature might differ. Individuals may have differing viewpoints on the ethical decisions made by the characters and the moral teachings given by the book.

POLITICS AND SOCIETY IN ITALY

Leon's writings are frequently used to attack Italian society and politics. She puts light on numerous social, cultural, and political themes that are prominent in Italy through her intriguing crime storylines and well-developed characters. Her sophisticated judgment shows her in-depth knowledge of the country, and she utilizes her novels to spark debate and create awareness about these concerns.

Leon's analysis is notable for its examination of corruption inside Italian institutions. Her novels typically highlight examples of corruption in law enforcement, government, and even the court system. Commissario Guido Brunetti frequently faces challenges and dilemmas as a result of the pervasive effect of corruption. Leon criticizes the systemic weaknesses and lack of responsibility within Italian institutions by spotlighting these shortcomings, delivering a compelling message about the importance of transparency and integrity.

The impact of organized crime, particularly the Mafia, on Italian society is another common theme in Leon's writings. She investigates the far-reaching impact of criminal organizations, and how they penetrate politics, economics, and everyday life. Leon's writings highlight the destructive potential of organized crime and the difficulties that law enforcement faces in tackling it. Her criticism is a call to action against criminal networks, emphasizing the necessity for greater measures to combat them.

Leon's works also address societal themes that are prevalent in Italian society. She speaks about racism, xenophobia, and social inequalities. She depicts incidents of discrimination suffered by marginalized people, mainly immigrants, in her works. Leon explores the preconceptions and biases embedded in Italian society via the experiences and interactions of her characters. Her critique emphasizes the necessity of empathy, compassion, and overcoming all types of discrimination.

In addition, Donna Leon's novels expose the environmental devastation caused by unregulated growth and tourism in Venice. She emphasizes the negative implications of mass tourism in her storytelling, such as the deterioration of local culture, the strain on infrastructure, and the destruction of natural habitats. Her criticism of unchecked development in tourist numbers highlights the critical need for sustainable practices and responsible tourism.

Leon's works address greater philosophical and ethical issues in addition to societal and political critiques. She discusses human responsibility, morals, and the moral quandaries that her characters endure. She encourages readers to consider their own values, decisions, and the impact they have on society through her storytelling.

In summary, Donna Leon's works feature a substantial critique of Italian culture and politics. She presents thought-provoking narratives that urge readers to reflect on Italy's concerns by tackling issues like as corruption, organized crime, social injustice, racism, and environmental degradation. Leon's astute analysis adds to a larger conversation on the need for change, reform, and social consciousness inside Italian society and beyond.

FEMINISM AND GENDER ROLE

Through her characters and their relationships, Donna Leon's works gently explore feminism and challenge established gender stereotypes. While Leon's writings are not expressly labeled as feminist literature, they frequently show strong female characters and shed light on the intricacies of gender dynamics in Italian society.

One of Leon's novels' most remarkable features is the representation of women in varied ways, both as protagonists and as secondary characters. Paola Falier, Commissario Guido Brunetti's wife, is a crucial character who breaks traditional gender stereotypes. Paola is a well-educated and clever woman who frequently engages in academic debates and expresses her feminist beliefs. Throughout the series, she questions cultural expectations of women and argues for equality. Paola's character reflects Leon's own feminist views, which she gently weaves into the story.

Leon also introduces female characters from all walks of life who question gender preconceptions. For example, strong and independent women in positions of power, such as Signorina Elettra Zorzi, the assistant to Vice-Questore Patta. Signorina Elettra is shown as a smart and forceful professional who effortlessly navigates the male-dominated police bureaucracy. Her portrayal demonstrates that women can achieve in traditionally male-dominated fields and challenge established power structures.

Moreover, Donna Leon's works usually address societal concerns affecting women, such as violence against women, objectification, and gender discrimination. Leon's experiences draw light on the disparities and injustices that women confront. In "About Face," for example, she investigates migrant women's exploitation and human trafficking. By tackling these subjects, Leon brings attention to real-world gender inequalities and creates a forum for feminist conversations.

Furthermore, Leon's works usually investigate the intersectionality of gender and other social issues. She includes conversations of class, color, and cultural backgrounds, which allows readers to evaluate how gender connects with various dimensions of identity. This method lends depth to her storytelling, allowing for a more nuanced understanding of the issues experienced by women from various backgrounds.

While feminism and gender roles are significant themes in Leon's works, it is crucial to highlight that her depiction of gender dynamics is not limited to women. She also investigates the pressures and expectations placed on male characters by traditional, patriarchal masculinity in Italian society. This extensive examination of gender roles provides readers with a thorough understanding of the complexity involved in negotiating conventional gender expectations.

In the end, Donna Leon's novels explore feminist themes and question traditional gender norms by presenting strong female characters, addressing gender disparities, and delving into the nuances of gender dynamics in Italian society. Leon inspires readers to ponder on problems such as gender discrimination, objectification, and the hardships experienced by women in various aspects of life through her thought-provoking writings. Her investigation of feminism extends beyond women to include an analysis of the effects of masculinity as well as broader social issues. Leon develops a deeper understanding of gender relations and facilitates dialogues about gender equality by addressing these subjects.

AN OVERVIEW OF THEMES AND IDEAS

Her writings frequently dive into many themes and ideas that she explores in her books. Here are some of the major topics and ideas found throughout Donna Leon's works:

> **Corruption and Power**

The study of corruption and misuse of power, notably within the Italian government and institutions, is a common theme throughout Leon's novels. She shines attention on society's dark underbelly and the problems faced by those who seek to defend justice through her stories.

> **Social Critique**

Leon's works frequently criticize societal issues such as political corruption, environmental degradation, and social inequality. She utilizes her novels as a platform to address these topics and to spark conversation and debate among her readers.

> **Ethics and Morality**

Another prominent topic in Leon's novels is the moral quandaries that her characters face. Commissario Brunetti is frequently caught between his responsibilities as a police officer and his personal sense of fairness. This examination of ethics and morals gives dimension to the stories while also raising critical concerns about what is right and wrong.

> **Culture and Historical Setting**

Leon's novels are profoundly steeped in Venice's culture and historical setting. She wonderfully describes the city's architecture, art, and traditions, creating a strong feeling of location for readers. Her use of cultural and historical references lends authenticity and depth to her tale.

> ## Family and Relationships

In addition to the crime investigations, Leon dives into her characters' personal lives, particularly Brunetti's family dynamics. She delves into the complexity of relationships, such as marriage, children, and friendship, giving her works a human touch.

> ## Environmental Concerns

Leon's concern for the environment is another common topic in her works. She frequently emphasizes the negative effects of pollution and industrialization on Venice's sensitive ecosystem, emphasizing the importance of environmental awareness and conservation.

> ## Consumerism Critique

Leon's works frequently criticize modern society's excessive consumerism and materialism. She presents characters that are motivated by avarice and worldly things, emphasizing the emptiness and moral rot that such pursuits may cause.

It should be noted that these topics and ideas are not exhaustive, as Donna Leon's works are multidimensional and offer a diverse spectrum of investigations. Each work has its own distinct set of themes.

CHAPTER 7

LIFE OUTSIDE THE PEN

PERSONAL LIFE AND PHILANTHROPY

Given her reputation for discretion, Donna Leon hasn't revealed much about her private life to the general public. However, she was born in Montclair, New Jersey, in the United States, on September 28, 1942, it is known. She was born and raised in New Jersey before making the journey to Venice, Italy, where she has lived since the 1980s.

As she frequently combines the special charm and ambiance of the city into her tale, Leon's love for Venice is clear in her books. She has talked about how she has a strong connection to Venice and how it has shaped her life and career. According to Leon, who loves Venice's history, architecture, and cultural legacy, she feels a sense of belonging there.

Throughout her career, Donna Leon has participated in a number of philanthropic activities. She is a fervent supporter of environmental protection efforts and has given money to groups working to safeguard Venice and the ecosystem around it. It is obvious that Leon is concerned about spreading awareness of environmental issues and encouraging sustainable practices given the environmental themes that are evident throughout her writings.

Leon has also taken part in campaigns to advance education and literacy. She has taken part in literary gatherings and book festivals all around the world, sharing her writing experiences and inspiring audiences of all ages to appreciate reading. Leon has helped to advance literacy and the value of books in society by her participation in these events.

Although Donna Leon maintains a somewhat discreet personal life, her charity activities show her dedication to the subjects she cares about. She has shown a desire to have an impact beyond her literary profession by supporting literacy programs and advocating for environmental conservation.

PERSONAL INTEREST AND HOBBIES

There isn't much information accessible regarding Donna Leon's interests and pastimes due to her secretive personality. But it is clear from her writings and public pronouncements that she has a great love for music, art, and literature.

It is obvious that Leon has a passion for reading because she is a successful novelist. In interviews, she has talked about how she enjoys reading and finds inspiration in a variety of literary works. Her broad knowledge of literature shines through in her novels, which frequently include references to classic authors and their works. Leon most likely spends a large amount of time reading and researching various literary genres.

Leon appears to be interested in art as well. Venice, with its rich cultural legacy, serves as a great source of inspiration for her works. Her work frequently includes evocative descriptions of the city's architecture, paintings, and sculptures. Leon's attention to detail and respect for the arts indicates that she may have a personal interest in visiting museums, galleries, and other cultural institutions.

Music is another significant component of Leon's life. In her novels, she regularly cites classical music, particularly the works of artists such as Mozart and Verdi. Leon has mentioned in interviews that she enjoys listening to music while writing, finding it both inspiring and soothing. It is possible that she has a diverse taste in music and appreciates various genres beyond classical.

Given her strong connection to Venice, it is also plausible that Leon enjoys exploring the city's culinary scene. Italian cuisine is renowned worldwide, and Venice offers a unique array of dishes and flavors. In her novels, Leon often includes descriptions of meals and local delicacies, suggesting that she may have an interest in food and gastronomy.

While specific details about Donna Leon's personal interests and hobbies may be scarce, her writings provide insight into the things she values and finds inspiration in. Literature, art, music, and the culinary world all appear to have an impact on her creative endeavors and her life in Venice.

INVOLVEMENT IN CHARITABLE CAUSES

Donna Leon's involvement in humanitarian activities is not well recorded because she prefers to keep her personal life secret. However, she has shown a limited devotion to philanthropy and social causes in a few cases.

One important cause backed by Leon is the protection and preservation of Venice. As a long-term inhabitant of the city, she has seen personally the environmental issues and risks that Venice faces, such as increasing sea levels and mass tourism. She has emphasized her concern for the city's future and the necessity for sustainable practices to secure its survival in interviews. Leon has contributed a portion of her book sales to organizations dedicated to protecting Venice's cultural legacy and ecosystem.

Leon has expressed an interest in animal welfare in addition to her support for Venice. She frequently includes topics about animal rights and maltreatment of animals in her works. This shows that she may have personal beliefs regarding the ethical treatment of animals and may support organizations working to protect them.

While these are just a few examples of Leon's humanitarian contributions, it is crucial to remember that she leads a private life and does not actively publicize her charitable activities. It's likely that she contributes to other causes or organizations behind the scenes, but this information is kept private.

Donna Leon's dedication to charity activities is consistent with her profound love for Venice and her wish to preserve its cultural history and environment. Her concern for ethical issues is reflected in her support for animal welfare. While the scope of her philanthropic work is unknown, it is clear that she uses her position as an author to promote awareness and contribute to issues that are important to her.

INVOLVEMENT IN ACTIVISM

Donna Leon's activity extends beyond her support for charity initiatives. She has utilized her platform as an author to bring attention to and throw light on a variety of social and political concerns throughout her career.

Corruption in the Italian government and legal system is a common issue in Leon's novels. She investigates the weaknesses and inequalities that exist inside these organizations through her fictional detective, Commissario Guido Brunetti. Leon draws attention to real-life concerns and urges readers to question and challenge the status quo by tackling these issues in her works.

70

She is also well-known for her critique of Italy's political scene. In interviews, she has expressed her dissatisfaction with the country's pervasive corruption and incompetence, which she says is impeding growth. She has been outspoken about her dissatisfaction with politicians who prioritize personal benefit over constituent well-being. Leon's writing strives to start debates and promote accountability among those in positions of power.

Leon has also been a supporter of environmental causes. Aside from her support for Venice's preservation, she has spoken out against pollution and the depletion of natural resources. She has emphasized the necessity of sustainable practices and the need for individuals and governments to accept responsibility for their environmental impact.

Her activism is not limited to her novels and interviews. She has taken part in public debates and conversations on a variety of themes, including politics, literature, and social issues. Her eagerness to participate in these discussions reflects her determination to use her voice and power to impact change.

It is important to note that Leon's activism is not restricted to Italy. She has spoken out against human rights violations and injustices around the world also. Her works, which frequently address issues of social inequity and prejudice, reflect her global viewpoint and concern for marginalized populations.

While Donna Leon's activism is not as well-known as her crime thrillers, her commitment to confronting societal concerns is clear in her work. She actively contributes to the discussion of significant social and political issues through her writing, public appearances, and philanthropic contributions. Leon exhibits the power of art and literature in promoting social justice by using her platform to raise awareness and advocate for change.

CHAPTER 8

ACHIEVEMENTS

RECOGNITION

As a writer, Donna Leon has received a great deal of accolades and recognition. Her development of the immensely popular Commissario Guido Brunetti series, which has amassed a devoted readership all over the world, is one of her most notable accomplishments. The series, which started with the release of "Death at La Fenice" in 1992, currently includes almost 30 books with Commissario Brunetti as the main character. All of the books are set in Venice.

Leon's books have received recognition for their gripping narratives, moody settings, and nuanced characters. Her talent for capturing the spirit of Venice and incorporating it into her stories has received high praise. Her novels have become synonymous with the city of Venice, and many readers regard them as an integral part of their Venetian experience, which serves as an example of her success.

Donna Leon has garnered various prizes and honors for her writing, in addition to the success of her novels. One of her most prominent accomplishments was winning the Crime Writers' Association Silver Dagger for Fiction in 2000 for her work "Friends in High Places." This renowned prize honors brilliance in crime fiction and demonstrates Leon's competence as a writer in the field.

Leon has also received honors for her services to Italian culture and literature. For her whole body of work, she received the Corine Literature Prize in Germany in 2003. This prize recognizes excellent literary contributions and authors who have had a significant impact on the literary world.

Her accomplishments go beyond trophies and recognition. Her books have been translated into numerous languages and have sold millions of copies around the world. This global success reflects her storytelling's universal appeal and the enduring popularity of her characters.

Furthermore, Donna Leon's influence goes beyond the sphere of literature. Her novels spawned a television series, "Commissario Brunetti," which aired from 2000 to 2019. The series, set in Venice and starring the character of Commissario Brunetti, cemented Leon's impact and reach even farther.

In conclusion, Donna Leon's biggest accomplishment is the invention of the immensely successful Commissario Guido Brunetti series, which has captivated readers all over the world. Her ability to capture the essence of Venice, as well as her brilliant narrative, has earned her a slew of honors and accolades. Leon's influence extends beyond the literary world, as her works have inspired a successful television series. Donna Leon has established herself as one of the most talented and prominent crime fiction writers of her time by her accomplishments.

IMPACTS AND RECEPTIONS

Donna Leon's literary reception and impact have been great and far-reaching. Her writings, particularly the Commissario Guido Brunetti series, have a devoted worldwide readership and have won significant recognition.

The admiration for Leon's engaging storytelling is one of the main features of her reception. Her books are renowned for their complex narratives, fully realized characters, and profound topics. Readers are sucked into the environment she creates, eagerly following Commissario Brunetti's investigations and developing a stake in the consequences. The fact that Leon was able to captivate readers on such a profound level is evidence of his writing prowess.

Another part of Leon's reception is her ambient setting, which has received a lot of attention. In her books, Venice, with its distinct beauty and history, acts as a character. Readers are immediately transported to the city's canals, palazzos, and undiscovered nooks thanks to Leon's rich descriptions, which evoke a real sense of location. This meticulous attention to detail has received much praise and has enhanced the immersive reading experience of her books.

The countless accolades and distinctions Leon has garnered throughout the course of her career show how influential she has been in the literary world. She has won numerous notable accolades, including the German Book Prize and the Swedish Martin Beck Award, in addition to the 2000 Crime Writers' Association Silver Dagger for Fiction. These honors not only emphasize her accomplishments as a crime fiction author but also her contributions to the field.

Additionally, Leon's contributions to Italian literature and culture have been honored. Her novels provide insights into Italian society, politics, and corruption, putting light on themes that are relevant to readers in and outside of Italy. Leon has established herself as an essential voice in contemporary Italian literature by combining these issues into her novels.

Leon's works' global success is yet another proof to her influence. Her books have sold millions of copies worldwide and have been translated into over 30 languages. This broad readership reflects her storytelling's worldwide appeal and the enduring popularity of her characters. Many readers regard Leon's works as a vital part of their Venetian experience, cementing her impact and extending even further.

Her influence can be observed outside of the literary realm in the television adaptations of her works. The "Commissario Brunetti" television series, which broadcast for nearly two decades, brought her characters to life on film and introduced her work to a new audience. This adaptation broadened Leon's audience and solidified her place as a leading figure in crime fiction.

Donna Leon's reception and impact as a writer have been substantial and far-reaching. Her ability to engage readers with fascinating writing, as well as her expert description of Venice, has earned her countless honors and accolades. Leon's influence extends beyond the literary world, with her works being translated into various languages, selling millions of copies, and inspiring a successful television series. Donna Leon has established herself as one of the most accomplished and prominent crime fiction authors of her time.

LEGACY

Donna Leon's legacy includes both her writing accomplishments and her activism. As an author, she has written a popular series of crime thrillers set in Venice that feature the astute investigator Commissario Guido Brunetti. Her books have received international recognition and have been translated into other languages, enthralling readers with their compelling plots and vividly created characters.

Leon's writing legacy is defined by her ability to flawlessly integrate thrilling crime novels with social critique. Her stories are more than just entertainment; they delve into the complexity of Italian society and expose its shortcomings. She illuminates themes such as corruption, inequality, and environmental degradation via her novels, forcing readers to confront hard facts.

One of Leon's legacies is her investigation of corruption in the Italian government and legal system. Her works provide a nuanced depiction of the difficulties experienced by those seeking justice in a system riddled with bribery, nepotism, and political influence. Leon challenges readers to examine the integrity of institutions and consider the consequences of corruption on society by confronting these concerns head on.

Her critique of the Italian political environment is also part of Leon's legacy. Her displeasure with politicians' incompetence and self-serving character is obvious in her interviews and public pronouncements. Leon encourages people to demand accountability and fight for a more transparent and ethical political system by expressing her dissatisfaction with those in power.

Leon's activist legacy also includes her support for environmental causes. Her affection for Venice and concern for its preservation shine through in her works, where she emphasizes the city's vulnerability to pollution and climate change. She emphasizes the relevance of sustainable practices and the necessity for individuals and governments to prioritize environmental stewardship in her writing and public appearances.

Donna Leon's work is also distinguished by her global outlook and sensitivity for marginalized populations. She uses her platform to bring attention to human rights violations and socioeconomic inequalities not just in Italy, but around the world. By incorporating themes of social inequality and discrimination into her novels, Leon fosters empathy and understanding among readers, encouraging them to confront systemic issues and work towards a more equitable society.

In addition to her literary accomplishments, Leon's legacy as an activist is distinguished by her desire to join in public dialogues and debates. Her involvement in these discussions illustrates her dedication to bringing about change outside the confines of her writings. Leon is a prime example of the ability of art and literature to advance social justice by leveraging her voice and influence.

As a whole, Donna Leon left behind a legacy of outstanding writing and advocacy. She engages readers with gripping tales in her crime novels while also tackling important social and political concerns. Her commitment to bringing about change, encouraging accountability, and fostering awareness solidifies her position as a writer and activist whose influence goes far beyond the written word.

CHAPTER 9

WRITING LEGACY

CONTRIBUTION TO THE LITERAL WORK

With her critically praised Commissario Guido Brunetti series and insightful social criticism, Donna Leon has had a tremendous impact on the literary world. Her novels have captured readers with their compelling plots, evocative images of Venice, and vividly written characters.

The lasting success of her Commissario Guido Brunetti series, which has spanned over thirty books, is one of Leon's finest achievements. Brunetti, a Venetian police investigator recognized for his knowledge, ethics, and compassion, is a beloved figure in this series. Brunetti's investigations into crimes frequently lead him to unearth corruption within the Italian government and court system, bringing light on the difficulties that those seeking justice face in a system riddled with bribery and political involvement. Readers have found this investigation into corruption to be compelling and value Leon's ability to address difficult social topics within the confines of a detective thriller.

Leon's novels also serve as a platform for her advocacy, as she weaves corruption, inequality, and environmental devastation into her stories. Her sophisticated depiction of these situations forces readers to confront painful social facts and motivates them to demand accountability. Her dissatisfaction with politicians' incompetence and self-serving attitude is clear in her interviews and public pronouncements, and she utilizes her writing to express her dissatisfaction and advocate for change.

Leon's affection for Venice and concern for its preservation may also be seen in her books. She emphasizes the city's susceptibility to pollution and climate change, emphasizing the importance of sustainable practices and environmental care. In doing so, she raises awareness of the importance of preserving Venice's unique cultural and natural heritage.

Her works are influenced by her global viewpoint and sensitivity for marginalized populations. She sheds attention on human rights violations and socioeconomic inequalities in Italy and around the world, encouraging readers to feel empathy and understanding. She encourages readers to examine systemic challenges and work towards a more equal society through her narratives.

Donna Leon's contributions to the literary world are considerable and diverse. Her Commissario Guido Brunetti mystery series has captivated readers, while her social commentary urges readers to examine societal issues. She has established her reputation as a writer and activist whose influence goes far beyond the written word through her activism and commitment to bringing attention to, fostering accountability for, and pushing for change.

FINAL THOUGHT ON ENDURING LEGACY

Donna Leon will be remembered for her ability to weave compelling narrative with social insight that will leave readers thinking. She has developed a lovable protagonist with her Commissario Guido Brunetti series who not only solves crimes but also highlights the inequities and corruption in the Italian political and judicial systems. Readers have responded favorably to this examination of societal concerns because they value Leon's ability to clarify complicated subjects within the confines of a crime fiction.

The activism of Leon is another important part of her legacy. She challenges readers to confront painful facts about society and demand accountability by addressing topics of corruption, inequality, and environmental damage in her works. Her determination to expressing her dissatisfaction and demanding change is clear in her interviews and public pronouncements, which highlight her disgust with politicians and their self-serving attitude.

Furthermore, it is clear from Leon's paintings that she adores Venice and cares deeply about its preservation. She emphasizes the significance of sustainable practices and environmental stewardship while highlighting the city's vulnerability to pollution and climate change. She does this to spread awareness about the significance of preserving Venice's distinctive natural and cultural heritage.

Leon's works are influenced by her global viewpoint and sensitivity for marginalized populations. She sheds attention on human rights violations and socioeconomic inequalities in Italy and around the world, encouraging readers to feel empathy and understanding. She encourages readers to examine systemic challenges and work towards a more equal society through her narratives.

To summarize, Donna Leon's lasting legacy is one of literary quality paired with a dedication to social activity. Her Commissario Guido Brunetti mystery series has captivated readers, while her social commentary urges readers to examine societal issues. She has confirmed her place as a writer and activist whose impact reaches far beyond the written word by her activism and dedication to raising awareness, encouraging accountability, and fighting for change. Her contributions to the literary world will be remembered and praised for many years to come.

LASTING IMPACT ON LITERATURE

Donna Leon's long-term influence on literature cannot be overestimated. She has not only captivated readers with fascinating crime novels set in Venice through her Commissario Guido Brunetti series, but she has also utilized her platform to confront critical social concerns and campaign for change. Her distinct combination of gripping storytelling, complex character development, and thought-provoking social commentary has cemented her place as a literary great.

One of the most important characteristics of Leon's literary influence is her ability to create vivid and authentic locations. In her works, Venice, with its labyrinthine canals, decaying beauty, and complicated social relationships, functions as a character in and of itself. Leon's thorough attention to detail and in-depth knowledge of the city's history and culture transport readers to its streets, squares, and hidden corners. She provides a feeling of place that enhances the overall reading experience by immersing readers in the particular ambiance of Venice.

Leon's lasting impact extends beyond the environment to her representation of diverse and nuanced individuals. The series' protagonist, Commissario Guido Brunetti, is not your standard detective. He is a caring family man who navigates the perilous seas of corruption and bureaucracy with honesty and a clear sense of fairness. Brunetti's moral compass and devotion to doing what is right, even if it means going against the grain, appeal to readers, making him a pleasant and engaging protagonist.

Beyond Brunetti, Leon skillfully develops the characters of the supporting cast as well, including his wife Paola, his coworkers at the police station, and the numerous people he meets while doing his investigations. Each character is multi-dimensional, with flaws, motivations, and personal difficulties of their own. Leon adds depth and complexity to her novels by diving into their lives and relationships, making them more than merely crime stories.

However, Leon's ability to smoothly incorporate social commentary into her works genuinely distinguishes her as a writer. She addresses a wide range of themes, such as governmental corruption, environmental degradation, socioeconomic injustice, and human rights violations. Her stories act as a mirror to society, highlighting its shortcomings and encouraging readers to challenge the established quo.

Leon's investigation into corruption in the Italian government and legal system is especially significant. She uncovers the insidious nature of bribery and political meddling in her works, focusing light on the difficulties experienced by individuals seeking justice in a corrupt system. Her sophisticated depiction of these challenges forces readers to confront painful social facts and encourages them to demand accountability.

Her critique of the Italian political scene adds another dimension of complexity to her art. Her writing reflects her dissatisfaction with politicians' incompetence and self-serving character, and she employs her books as a platform to express her dissatisfaction and demand change. She invites readers to reflect on their own complacency and actively participate in reshaping the future by revealing the system's shortcomings.

Donna Leon's interest for environmental preservation has had a lasting influence on literature in addition to her work within Italy. Her novels reflect her passion for Venice and commitment to educating readers about the city's exposure to pollution and climate change. She highlights the critical need for sustainable practices and invites readers to consider their own duty to the earth by infusing environmental issues into her novels.

Last but not least, Leon's understanding of the world and compassion for underprivileged groups have enhanced her influence on writing. She exposes societal inequalities and violations of human rights, both in Italy and other countries, through her novels. She encourages readers' empathy and understanding by giving a voice to individuals who are frequently marginalized, which encourages them to address structural problems and work towards a more fair society.

Finally, Donna Leon's ability to weave gripping narrative with social commentary has left a lasting impression on literature. She has crafted a universe that enthralls readers through her Commissario Guido Brunetti series while addressing important themes like corruption, inequality, and environmental devastation. Her place as a literary giant, whose influence goes well beyond the written word, has been cemented by her rigorous attention to detail, intricate character development, and commitment to action. It is certain that Donna Leon's legacy will continue to influence and inspire both the criminal genre and literature as a whole as people eagerly anticipate her upcoming books.

CONCLUSION

U ltimately, this iconic biography of the pen queen of Venice is a monument to her extraordinary life and achievements. It examines the many dimensions of her legacy, such as her capacity to weave compelling narratives with provocative social critique. She has developed a lovable protagonist with her Commissario Guido Brunetti series which not only solves crimes but also highlights the inequities and corruption in the Italian political and judicial systems.

Another important part of Leon's legacy is her activism since she uses her books as a platform to talk about issues like corruption, inequality, and environmental destruction. In her interviews and public remarks, she has made it clear how committed she is to expressing her dissatisfaction with lawmakers and urging change. Leon promotes social awareness and action by urging readers to confront hard societal facts and demand accountability.

Additionally, Leon's devotion to Venice and concern for its preservation are visible in all of her paintings. She emphasizes the significance of sustainable practices and environmental stewardship while highlighting the city's vulnerability to pollution and climate change. She spreads awareness about the importance of preserving Venice's distinctive natural and cultural legacy through her narratives.

As she exposes societal injustices and violations of human rights in Italy and throughout the world, Leon's works are influenced by her global vision and concern for marginalized populations. She motivates readers to address structural problems and work towards a more equal society by creating empathy and understanding among her audience.

In conclusion, Donna Leon's biographical book provides a thorough examination of her ongoing legacy. It demonstrates her writing talent as well as her devotion to social activism. Her contributions to the literary world will be cherished and treasured for years to come, as her intriguing mysteries and thought-provoking social commentary continue to capture readers and encourage change.